How to Scale Your Business to $10-$100 Million

Danny Breadmaker

Newsletter

Our complimentary weekly newsletter delivers insights to help entrepreneurs grow their companies into the $10-$100 million range. Through the newsletter, we share actionable strategies and valuable knowledge about scaling businesses to their fullest potential.

Once you join, you will receive a brand new free eBook release every month.

Join our newsletter to stay up-to-date on scientifically proven tactics that can expand your business today.

You can join at https://dannybreadmaker.beehiiv.com/subscribe.

Contents

One

Entering New Lands of Opportunity

Every business begins by serving a local customer base. But the biggest companies extend far beyond their hometowns. Expanding your geographic reach and entering new markets is a proven path to growth.

When Harry's Razors launched in 2013, they focused on winning over American consumers with their subscription shaving model. Within a few years, they turned their sights north and acquired a Canadian e-commerce platform to gain a foothold internationally. Soon Harry's was tailoring their marketing and operations specifically for Canadians, translated into French and partnering with local retailers.

The international team faced regulatory hurdles shipping their product internationally and adapting their U.S.-focused branding for local sensitivities. But within two years Harry's commanded over 5% market share in Canada. And their cross-border expansion was just beginning.

Like Harry's Razors, your business can tap into new waves of demand by strategically entering other geographic markets. But it requires in-depth preparation.

You'll need to research each market extensively - the competitive landscape, growth projections, operational and legal requirements, business culture and consumer preferences. Don't just translate your messaging and products. Adapt them to local norms.

Hiring local teams is ideal to gain insider understanding. Partner with well-connected figures in each market to build trust and relationships. Be ready to invest substantially upfront before reaping expansion rewards.

Beyond geography, your own customer base holds segmentation opportunities. Identify underserved groups you can better attract. Turn general messaging into targeted appeals. Meet their unique needs with tailored offerings.

Finally, don't limit your distribution pipelines. Pursue omni-channel distribution suited to your product. Pilot new channels in small settings first. Integrate operations across channels to align inventory, pricing and the customer experience.

Expanding your markets takes upfront investment but holds transformational potential. The broader your business's reach, the greater its rewards. Venture beyond familiar shores, and growth awaits.

Two

Spreading the Word Through Strategic Marketing

In the early days of launching a business, marketing often takes a backseat to product development and operations. But once you achieve product-market fit, it's time to step on the gas and amplify your message.

Strategic marketing provides the fuel for growth by spreading awareness of your brand to the masses. It establishes your company as a household name that customers can trust.

Consider the meteoric rise of Peloton. After creating a high-end exercise bike paired with streaming classes, they invested heavily in brand building. Peloton's aspirational messaging focused on self-improvement, community and empowerment.

Their polished ads helped position Peloton as a luxury fitness brand. The company also pursued retail partnerships, showroom expansion and earned media opportunities. This marketing muscle propelled Peloton's growth to over 5.4 million members within 8 years.

To achieve this scale, you can't just post social media and hope people organically discover you. You need an integrated strategy combining brand building, digital marketing, influencer partnerships and more.

First, clearly define your brand identity through logo, design language, messaging pillars and personality. Immerse customers at every touchpoint - site, packaging, retail - with sensory brand cues.

Next, create viral content designed for organic sharing and paid promotion. Videos, memes, contests and challenges allow you to engage at scale.

Build relationships with relevant influencers - nano to mega - who can authentically convey your brand story. Offer creative compensation models to align incentives.

And don't forget the power of traditional channels like public relations and event sponsorships. Look for brand alignment over pure reach.

With large growth comes increased competition. A strategic marketing engine ensures customers continue choosing you amidst endless options. Spread your message far and wide, and they will come.

Three

Optimizing Operations for Growth

In the early startup days, operations often take a backseat to product and sales. But sustainable growth requires smooth, scalable operations. Otherwise, more customers mean more problems.

Bottlenecks turn into total gridlock. Inventory runs dry. Customers split for competitors. Quality crumbles under pressure. And it all threatens your growth trajectory.

Scaling requires systematically eliminating waste, delays and errors from your operations. The Japanese term "kaizen" meaning continuous improvement is the mindset needed.

Start by ruthlessly mapping workflows end-to-end. Prune unnecessary steps. Standardize processes. Decentralize decisions. Apply project management rigor.

Next, automate repetitive tasks through software, scripts and machine learning. Let technology handle high-volume activities while your team focuses on high-value work.

Strengthen your supply chain against disruptions. Boost procurement power through volume discounts. Locate facilities based on proximity to suppliers and markets.

Make decisions based on real-time operational data, not gut instinct. Quantify tradeoffs between options. Model scenarios to stress test growth plans.

Operations excellence won't appear in your marketing copy. But it allows you to deliver on the promises you make to customers time and time again.

Smooth operations means no bad surprises - just happy customers and sustained success. Don't let operations become the invisible ceiling to your growth. Optimize them continuously, and the sky's the limit.

Four

Expanding Your Offerings to Customers

The most direct path to growth is providing more value to your customers. Give them more of what they want, and they will give you more business.

This starts by intimately understanding customer needs and desires. Directly ask your best customers what problems they still face. Where are they underserved? Obsess over their pain points.

Armed with these insights, ideate new offerings aligned to your brand and capabilities. Seek adjacent spaces you can expand into. Develop minimum viable products to rapidly test concepts.

Don't just create one-off products. Structure them into bundled solutions that provide greater convenience and value. Offer tiered bundles tailored to different customer segments.

Subscription pricing models also cultivate loyal, recurring revenue streams. But you must truly enhance value over time - not just lock customers in. Subscriptions are continued by earning renewals.

As you expand offerings, double down on your highest-lifetime-value customers. Nurture them with perks, personalized promotions and dedicated account managers.

Leveraging your current customers and expertise for expansion is faster and lower risk than constantly acquiring brand new customers.

So before chasing excessive product breadth or straying too far from your core competencies, reflect on who you can further serve. Deepen your relationship with customers, and growth will follow.

Five

Growing Through Strategic Partnerships

Forming strategic partnerships can be a powerful way to scale your business. Partnerships allow you to expand capabilities and reach new markets faster than going it alone.

Pursuing co-marketing partnerships with complementary brands can provide valuable exposure to new audiences. Seek out partners with similar values, positioning, and target demographics. Develop integrated campaigns and content together that leverages both brands. This could include promotions, contests, sweepstakes, and sponsorships aimed at generating buzz and conversions. The costs of campaign production, media buys, and event sponsorships can be split between partners. Each partner should leverage their own audience and marketing channels for further reach. It's important to ensure consistent messaging across the joint efforts. The partnership results can be tracked against KPIs like website traffic, email sign-ups, sales referrals and more.

Establishing channel partnerships helps expand sales and distribution reach. Potential partners should be evaluated on their capabilities, reputation and reach. A partnership opportunity can be pitched as a win-win, with negotiated terms on revenue share, territories, activities and timeframes. Partners need training on your products and how to best position the value to customers. Equipping partners with branded assets, demo tools, and marketing materials enables them to better promote your products. Incentives can be offered for hitting key sales volume and performance milestones. Ongoing communication and feedback elicitation is crucial to maximize the opportunity over time.

Technology partnerships enable gaining capabilities faster than developing in-house. First identify holes and opportunities for improvement in your platform or products. Research startups with innovative, complementary technologies that could address those gaps. Frame the partnership as a way to jointly build better solutions through integration. For example, combining APIs can lead to seamless customer experiences. New products can also be co-developed together. Cross-promotional activities and co-marketing leverages both companies' strengths. Partnerships serve as social proof and validation when selling to customers. If successful over an extended period, explore acquisition potential.

To maximize strategic partnerships, ensure both sides' incentives are aligned toward the shared objectives. Maintain regular communication cadences, share data and insights, and treat the partner like an extension of your own team. Co-develop processes for smooth interoperability. Participate in each other's events, marketing initiatives and

PR opportunities. Express appreciation and publicly recognize major accomplishments.

Forging strategic win-win partnerships accelerates growth by combining strengths and minimizing go-it-alone risk. But alignment, communication and flawless execution are vital to fully capitalize on the opportunity.

Six

Fueling Growth Through Mergers and Acquisitions

Pursuing mergers and acquisitions (M&A) can rapidly accelerate the growth of a company. Acquiring or merging with complementary businesses allows you to expand into new markets and gain technologies faster than building organically. But successfully executing M&A is complex.

First, you need to identify acquisition targets that strategically fill capability and market gaps for your business. Profile characteristics of your ideal target such as market, product offerings, reputation, culture, talent, and technology assets. Thoroughly research candidates and model out valuation and deal structure scenarios.

Conduct extensive due diligence on any potential deal. Review financials, growth projections, contracts, customer data, IP, and legal liabilities. Visit facilities in person and interview management. Build an integration plan identifying synergies in operations, distribution, and costs. Quantify any risks and make sure the opportunity aligns to your strategy.

Carefully negotiate deal terms that are equitable to both parties. Structure agreements using cash, stock, and earn-outs tied to performance. Develop a detailed integration roadmap and communicate the vision to employees. Prioritize high-value synergies for early integration focus.

Post-close, retain key talent from the acquired company and clarify roles across leadership. Consolidate business functions and streamline overlapping processes. Blend company cultures by connecting teams to the shared mission. Manage complex technology and system integrations smoothly.

Measure results against identified synergies and growth opportunities. Communicate progress frequently and address concerns. M&A can have huge upside, but requires meticulous planning and skilled execution. With the right approach, it can be a rocket ship to reaching the next level.

Seven

Building an A-Team to Drive Growth

Having a high-performing team is critical for scaling a business. An A-player workforce with complementary strengths will out-execute any competitors. Recruiting, developing and retaining top talent must be a priority.

To attract top talent, be clear on must-have skills, experience and culture fit. Leverage networks and recruiters to source qualified candidates. Showcase your company mission, culture and growth opportunities. Assess problem-solving abilities and emotional intelligence in addition to technical competencies. Compensate competitively and customize offers. Sell the vision and development potential to close candidates.

Once on board, identify skill and knowledge gaps to tailor training programs. Offer access to online courses, seminars, certifications and conferences. Facilitate mentorships and coaching with experienced employees. Give stretch assignments, job rotations and special projects to accelerate development. Create individualized employee development plans.

Retaining and motivating top talent is then crucial. Check in regularly on satisfaction and feedback. Provide opportunities for career growth through clear promotion paths and increased responsibility. Maintain competitive pay benchmarked to your industry. Spotlight contributions and tie to company success.

Building an unstoppable team requires instilling a shared sense of purpose and culture. Attract those aligned to your values. Promote diversity of backgrounds and perspectives. Empower people with trust and autonomy. Maintain a flat organization open to ideas from all levels. Celebrate wins frequently.

With a world-class team, you can accomplish exponentially more than the sum of individual efforts. So don't underspend on the talent required to get there. Your people ultimately determine how high your business can climb.

Eight

Funding Growth at Each Stage

Accessing sufficient capital is vital to scale rapidly. Different funding options match the needs at different stages of growth.

In the earliest days, bootstrapping by minimizing costs and leveraging founder resources is wise. Launch with a minimum viable product using lean distribution channels. Tighten payment terms and get by with minimal inventory. Consider founder loans to bridge short-term gaps.

Seeking venture capital investment makes sense once you achieve product-market fit and want to accelerate growth. Identify VC firms focused on your space and research their prior investments. Perfect your pitch conveying large market potential, competitive advantages, and traction. Respond quickly and professionally to due diligence. Negotiate valuation and terms founder-friendly. Leverage VC expertise and connections.

Preparing for an initial public offering requires getting audit-ready financials, bolstering management, and timing to market conditions. Hire an experienced investment bank to guide the process. File S-1 registration and work through SEC review. Market the company story through non-deal roadshows and media. Price shares based on investor demand signals. Use IPO proceeds to fund expansion.

At all stages, manage capital responsibly. Allocate to the highest-return activities first. Balance growth with profit focus. Maintain adequate reserves and limit dilution. Demonstrate ROI on investments to investors. Remain nimble to adjust plans based on conditions. Keep investors informed through transparency.

The exact path and timing varies, but accessing the necessary capital at each phase of growth is key to scaling up. Treat funding as fuel to accelerate expansion, not as an end in itself.

Nine

Designing Scalable Processes and Operations

Scaling a business requires intentionally designing processes and operations to support increased volume. Planning must happen across production, fulfillment, customer service, quality control and organizational structure.

To scale production and fulfillment, analyze capacity needed to meet demand forecasts. Add shifts, expand facilities and streamline workflows. Balance in-house and outsourced manufacturing. Implement just-in-time inventory management. Automate production systems with the latest technology. Standardize components for flexibility. Ensure quality control across expanded output. Optimize distribution networks and logistics routes.

Providing scalable customer service starts with launching chatbots for frequent basic inquiries and robust self-service resources. Track customer satisfaction (CSAT) metrics. Build a tiered support model with specialized roles to handle more complex issues. Hire and train support staff ahead of projected need. Implement customer relationship management (CRM) to standardize processes and workflows.

Maintaining quality standards requires documenting procedures thoroughly. Identify key control points across workflows. Collect production and operations metrics. Build a culture with quality ownership at all levels. Leverage automation to reduce defects. Address systemic gaps through continuous process improvements.

Finally, evaluate and evolve organizational structure for scale. Hire executives with experience scaling companies. Plan for succession of key positions. Maintain culture amidst growth through communication. Break down silos between teams. Decentralize authority appropriately. Promote transparency.

While scaling brings growing pains, careful preparation of processes and operations reduces disruption. The best growth maintains quality standards and customer satisfaction. With the right systems in place, a company's reach can expand exponentially.

Ten

Managing Rapid Growth

Rapidly scaling a business brings an exciting set of challenges. Leadership, culture, priorities and processes all need to evolve to support massive growth.

As a company grows, leadership responsibilities must be clearly defined across the executive team and board. Hire or promote experienced executives into key roles, ensuring continuity of vision and values. Set up management training and mentoring. Craft individualized development plans for high-potentials. Maintain open communication around organizational changes.

Preserving company culture amid growth is crucial. Articulate core cultural values, mission and purpose early on. Reinforce those values in hiring, onboarding and reviews. Decentralize decision-making to reinforce trust. Promote cross-department collaboration. Celebrate wins, milestones and employee successes often. Encourage open dialogue and feedback at all levels. Stay grounded in roots through growth phases.

Setting priorities and growth goals keeps everyone aligned. Develop 3-5 year strategic plans balancing short and long-term objectives. Prioritize must-have capabilities. Set specific, measurable goals by department tied to incentives. Maintain focus on primary revenue drivers. Re-forecast regularly based on latest assumptions.

Sustaining momentum requires tracking customer satisfaction and employee engagement. Celebrate wins but remain ambitious. Cascade priorities clearly across management levels. Maintain agility to flex plans based on market feedback. Keep innovating on customer experience. Continually reinforce vision and rally the team. Manage the rollercoaster with steady leadership.

Rapid growth is thrilling but requires thoughtful orchestration across many facets of an organization. With smart leadership and strategic prioritization, surging demand can be harnessed to reach full potential.

Eleven

Your Scale-Up Journey Awaits

We've explored the key areas to scale your business in this book - from expanding into new markets to honing operations, strategically funding growth, and managing rapid scaling. While every company's path is unique, some common themes apply:

Pursuing growth requires balancing long and short-term thinking. You need to map out an ambitious vision for the future while executing incremental expansion in the present. Maintaining this dual focus is tricky but critical.

As you scale, operational excellence and customer experience can never be sacrificed, even amidst chaos. Obsess over maintaining quality standards and satisfaction levels throughout growth phases.

Securing the right capital needs to happen at each stage, but funding should be treated as a means to an end goal, not the end goal itself. Avoid pursuing growth for growth's sake alone.

Partnerships and mergers & acquisitions can catapult progress much faster than going it alone. But they require flawless execution and alignment to maximize the opportunity. Assess risks thoroughly.

Building a high-performing team makes everything possible. Recruiting, retaining and developing top talent across your organization should remain an utmost priority.

With increased scale comes greater complexity. Management rigor, systems and processes need to evolve to prevent fragmentation.

Stay nimble and adaptable to changing market conditions, while remaining steadfast in your core strategy. Pivoting too frequently dilutes focus.

And importantly, celebrate wins frequently to maintain momentum. Scaling is a rollercoaster - enjoy the thrill of the ride.

Scaling a business is not for the faint of heart. But by learning from those before you, playing to your core strengths, and surrounding yourself with an amazing team, you can turn ambitious growth goals into reality.

I hope this book has demystified key steps on the scale-up journey and sparked ideas for your business. The world needs more bold entrepreneurs pursuing big visions. Wishing you the best as you continue your adventure!